BLEACHER BUDDIES

By
Patricia L. Bortnem

Illustrations by
E. Terry Roisum

Enjoy!
Pat Bortnem

United States Copyright Office.
Library of Congress Registration # Txu 908-360

ISBN 0-9679079-0-X

Printed in the United States of America
Moberly's Print Shop
Sioux Falls, SD 57104-0341

About the Author...

Pat Bortnem is a Registered Nurse with a Masters Degree in Education who teaches at Southeast Technical Institute is Sioux Falls, SD. She was raised in Ames, IA and has lived her entire adult life in South Dakota. It is a life in which sporting activities provide a great deal of social interaction with a number of different people. Pat is a woman who loves people of all ages, and enjoys observing and getting to know them. One usually knows if Pat is around as she is in the group that is laughing, talking and enjoying. Over the years, she has written many poems for people to celebrate special occasions. She is aware that although these poems are by no means literary masterpieces, they do allow people to relate to common feelings and share some laughter.

Dedication

This book is dedicated to my children, Jason, Angie and Nick, who are the reasons I became a "bleacher buddy" in the first place. Watching them in sporting events gave me a true sense of pride and was a very important and memorable part of my life. They have given me hours of entertainment and activity throughout all the aspects of their years at home and on the run. Thanks, kids! My most frequent bleacher buddy was my husband, Alan, and I will treasure the memories of the good times together on the bleachers. He has also been extremely supportive in my many endeavors. Thanks, Al!

This book is also dedicated to my many bleacher buddies throughout the years and the many sports. The poems are intended to reflect the different personalities of people with whom I have shared the bleachers over the years. I wrote them in support of all the people who get out and cheer on the children in their lives. They are not intended to target any one person or necessarily any one sport. Please enjoy them in the fun spirit in which they are intended and share them with your own bleacher buddies.

ACKNOWLEDGEMENTS:

TO: My parents, who always have had, and continue to have a huge influence on my life. I am very grateful to them for allowing me so many experiences and for loving me always.

TO: Terry Roisum for giving so generously of his talents of music, art and humor, and to his wife, Dianne for sharing him.

TO: My family members, sisters, brothers, in-laws, nieces, and nephews who mean the world to me.

TO: My coworkers, past and present, who have encouraged me on a daily basis, and made a fuss over the poems.

TO: My friends and neighbors for all the times we have been there for each other.

TO: My students, past and present, who energize me.

TO: Children everywhere who are so fun to listen to and watch.

TABLE OF CONTENTS

GUM

New Buddies

Ours was the new kid on the team,
We didn't know a soul.
We sat lonely on the bleachers,
Trying to figure out our role.

I was looking at the folks around,
For a mom like me to meet.
One who'd fill me in on things,
And join me for something to eat.

To get someone to visit with,
I didn't have to beg.
I turned to a woman to say "hello,"
And my gum fell on her leg.

"I'm sorry — excuse me please,
I'm not off to a very good start."
She looked at me and started to laugh,
It was a laugh that came from the heart.

We've been friends ever since that day,
Our kids have played many a game.
My bleacher buddies are very dear to me,
And it seems no two are the same.

CLINIC PHYSICAL
SCHEDULE
PRACTICE Dates
AUGUST
SIGN-IN SHEET

Getting Ready

We are having a special meeting,
To kick off the season.
There are sign-in sheets, etc.,
And forms for every reason.

Permission slips need signing,
All blanks must be filled out.
Physical forms must be completed,
And there will be a cost—no doubt!

Days are announced for practices,
And dates are set for games.
Schedules are handed out,
Lists of players and parent's names.

Occasionally there will be a "talk",
By a parent or a coach.
A reminder of good sportsmanship,
And behavior above reproach.

There are great hopes for the coming year,
Expectations are high.
Tournaments and match-ups,
And reaching for the sky.

In Style

There's a woman on the bleachers,
Who is styled like a magazine ad.
She is wondering how I so early in the day,
Can manage to look so bad.

She sits primly on the bleachers,
With every hair in place.
Her clothes are perfectly fitting,
As is the makeup on her flawless face.

How can she look so cool and crisp,
When I'm wilting like old lettuce.
Most of us are showing the wear of the day,
While she looks perfect—we won't let it get us.

I might as well go say "hello,"
Though I'm rumpled, sweaty and hot.
The contrast between our looks is huge,
But the contrast in caring is not.

We both care deeply about our kids,
I think to myself with a smile.
We laugh and share victories and losses,
Supporting kids is always in style.

STATS

Informed Fan

If you sit next to this gal,
You'll get statistics as well as the score.
She knows all about each team member,
Their weaknesses and more.

No distractions are allowed,
She's serious about the game.
If things are not going well,
She knows just who to blame.

She's even aware of the other team.
Who is good and who is not.
She looks at me as if I'm insane,
When I say, "What's the score, I forgot."

She goes over every play,
Long after the game is done.
"We had some bad calls. Where were their heads?
We should have had that one!"

Do not sit beside her,
If you don't want to watch the game.
Definitely never ever admit,
That you don't know each player's name.

Munchie Time

Some people come to the game,
With an impressive assortment of snacks.
Their bag is filled with salty and sweet,
And beverages in six packs.

The coolers and bags are everywhere
They take up bleacher space.
There's enough food for players and parents,
To continuously stuff their face.

Sunflower seeds are flying,
The munching has begun.
Between bites we still can yell,
"WE'RE NUMBER ONE!"

"Do you want me to bring you anything,
From the concession stand?
How about a hot dog or pretzel,
Or a large pop for each hand?"

Our diet leaves something to be desired,
When we hit the gym or park.
We share popcorn, candy and power drinks,
From morning until dark.

Loud and Proud

This person is so embarrassing,
Her voice is really loud,
She hollers at officials and players,
And stands out in the crowd.

Her kid's the one who's wincing,
As she has much advice to shout.
"Get under it, Get busy,
Look at the sidelines—it was out!"

She knows more than the officials,
More than the coaches, too.
You just have to ask her,
And she will make that clear to you.

She has this special war whoop,
She uses after good plays.
We may hear it 30 times,
On one of those really good days.

Her volume keeps increasing,
She is on her own.
She starts out with a crowd around her,
And ends up sitting alone.

Bleacher Buddies

Bleacher Buddies near and dear,
What a collection of friends!
We've shared highs and lows of many sports,
Jokes and tired rear ends!

We've had to endure the weather,
Cold and heat and storms.
We've huddled and shared our coffee,
Waiting for kids to perform.

We go from season to season,
The faces of the people change.
All pulling together for the kids
The collection of folks seems strange.

There are laborers, salespeople, professionals,
There's high income and low.
It's amazing how differences are set aside,
And how close to each other we grow.

Bleacher Buddies are people with class,
They're a one and only crowd.
And to be spending time together,
Makes them very proud!

What a Hoot!

This woman is a riot,
She always cracking jokes.
She has a comment for everyone,
The players and the folks.

I always try to sit next to her,
She's good for a sagging spirit.
The things that are the funniest,
She says so that only I can hear it.

My kid says I don't pay attention,
I just visit and laugh with "her."
Whether I come to see every detail of the game,
Or renew my humor, I'm not sure.

She's the one who keeps it positive,
Even when all hope is lost.
When the coach makes a dumb decision,
Or our "star of the game" gets tossed.

Even when we've lost a close one,
Or one we were sure we'd win.
She can say the thing to cheer us up,
And get the sourest among us to grin.

42
12

Riding the Pine

Many parents feel the hurt,
Of a child who doesn't play.
They continue to bring them to the game,
And to practice every day.

Maybe this game will be the one,
That the coach will choose them to play.
Maybe they'll even do something so well,
Like come in and save the day.

"Don't let them get hurt, don't let them screw up,"
It is every parent's prayer.
"Just let them get some playing time,
Let them be of help somewhere."

"It's only a game" and "Maybe next time,"
Are constantly repeated.
Especially when their heartbroken child,
Feels hurt and badly defeated.

"Riding the pine"—on the bench,
Builds character they say.
We'll be there at the next game,
And hope to heck they play.

3
22

Player Down

The tension mounts—a player is down,
"Can you see who it is?" I hear.
"Don't let it be serious; don't let it be mine,
Are they out for the rest of the year?"

A rising sense of panic,
As the crowd around them grows.
I promised never to come on the field,
I may break down today. Who knows?

"Why did I consent to this?
Who thought up this crazy sport?"
My mind is racing with possibilities
Of injuries of every sort.

It amazes me how something so fun,
Can suddenly turn so grim.
Thoughts of scoring and heroes,
Turn to thoughts of life and limb.

The player's up—a sigh of relief,
Being helped, but walking off the field!
I just smile as if in control,
But my fears have been revealed.

FAN

Loyal Fan

There is a guy that we all know,
He's a real familiar man.
He knows the kids, he knows the sport,
He's our most loyal fan.

He's yelling from the heart,
He's there at every game.
Though his kids are long since grown,
He's cheering just the same.

You can really count on him,
To encourage and suggest.
He calls out plays, he claps and shouts,
He thinks our team's the best.

Where does this person come from?
Why does he take the time?
To cheer on someone else's kids,
Did he play some in his prime?

A team can really use him,
He's there through thick and thin.
He'll be back at the next game,
Whether we lose or win.

BLEACHER
BUDDIES
FINANCIAL
STATEMENT

Keeping Busy

There is a group of women,
Who meet at every game.
It quickly becomes a working event,
The order is always the same.

They bring their latest project,
To work on when not at play.
Maybe needlework or reading,
Or a stack of bills to pay.

We're even seeing laptops,
Make their way to bleacher seats.
The keys are flying madly,
Through victories and defeats.

They may enlist your help,
Or ask you for your aid.
If you are close and willing,
It's the way new friends are made.

People choose to spend their time,
In a variety of ways.
Their hands are never idle,
On those long old tournament days.

RAFFLE
COUPONS
FUNDRAISER

Fundraisers

The big fundraising project,
Will be announced today.
No matter how you slice it,
We are all going to pay.

There's candy bars and coupon books,
For selling door to door.
There's a car wash Saturday morning,
Bake sales, carnivals, and more.

The kids from the opposing team,
Are selling magazines.
We're competing for the customers,
With wreaths and Christmas greens.

Our team is selling tickets,
To raffle a big TV.
There are prizes for top sellers,
Starting early is the key.

To tell the truth it's very hard,
To ask friends and family to buy.
I'd frankly rather write a check,
Because fundraisers make me cry.

12
9
3
6

Not Having Fun Yet

This particular person,
Really hates this sport.
She detests the action and the breaks,
And has worries of every sort.

She doesn't understand it,
How it's played or how it's scored.
She's just putting in her time,
She's upset and she is bored.

"Why does this have to take so long?"
I hope we lose so we can go.
Her attitude is very poor,
But she's hurting more than we know.

She's afraid her child will be upset,
She's afraid that he'll get hurt.
She's afraid of disappointment,
She's afraid he'll rip his shirt.

She needs comfort and encouragement,
She needs to understand the reason.
Her child keeps coming back to play,
Whatever sport's in season!

Picture This

This parent takes pictures of the kids,
Every time they make a move.
Actions and stills, good days and bad,
Whether they do or don't approve.

"Come on everyone, get together," she says,
"We'll take one alone and one of the group."
"Come on now, let's all smile,
Hey—don't be such a poop!"

People always talk about it,
"I'm glad I'm not that kid!"
But when we ask who got a perfect shot,
You can bet on it—she did!

She even gets the parents on film,
Players, coaches and officials, too.
You're just not safe with this shutter-bug here,
The pictures may come back to haunt you.

There is photographic evidence
And the pictures are the reason.
We have so much fun looking back,
At good times throughout the season.

Up and About

There are some fans who never sit,
Their buns don't touch the bleachers.
They pace and wander; they're up and down,
They are very restless creatures.

One minute you see them standing there,
You think they've picked a spot.
The next they're travelling all around,
Now they're settled—now they're not!

It seems this group is antsy,
From the minute they arrive.
They go from end to end with plays,
It's on moving that they thrive.

Why does it bother those who sit,
From arrival until it's done.
To watch some one go up and down,
To prefer being on the run.

Together we can appreciate,
The differences in us all.
Whether it's busy behavior or settled,
Everyone can have a ball.

Official Word

You get to know officials,
When you've been at a sport awhile.
Some are there to make you mad,
And some can really make you smile.

"I don't care if they're always right,
As long as they're consistent."
If they favor just one team,
The outcries are persistent.

When a team is losing,
The officials are to blame.
And when they just can't get a break,
They blame it on the same.

I've seen arrogant and cocky,
Sincere, as well as dedicated.
Those that should be in the Hall of Fame,
And those that should be medicated.

No matter how you slice it,
Officials work very hard.
They really need player and fan support,
And should be held in high regard.

Coaches

Coaches are every type and description
From expert to parent-recruit.
Some are themselves in tip-top shape,
Some more than fill out a sweat suit.

The kids have had the "screamer",
Whose voice scares even fans.
Who can be heard from goal to goal,
From sidelines to concession stands.

The coach who is the silent type,
Leaves many things unsaid.
But you get the message loud and clear,
From veins bulging from his head.

There are coaches who are nurturing,
Who always strive to understand.
They are the model of sportsmanship,
They demonstrate what they demand.

Whether positive or negative,
Coaches have a huge influence on lives.
Their behavior makes the difference,
Whether one thrives or just survives.

Carpool

Today is the day I really dread,
The day I drive the carpool.
I pick up kids all over town,
What am I—a fool?

This one forgot their sneakers,
Another their permission slip.
If one more kid's not ready when I come,
I'm really going to flip.

Sometimes it is very wild,
And many times it's fun.
Talking, laughing and complaining,
From beginning until it's done.

Seems I spend more time in the car,
Than I ever do in the house.
When will I cook a meal again,
Or spend any time with my spouse?

I can't wait until these kids can drive,
To practices on their own.
Wait a minute—on second thought,
That's a time I'm glad to postpone.

On a Date

I had a childless person ask me,
Where'd you go on your last date?
I attended a child's sporting event,
Don't worry, it was great!

This is where I meet my honey,
This is where we rendezvous.
Bleachers of metal, wood or cement,
A hot dog and a pop or two.

At times we're sweating bullets,
At times we're calm and cool.
At times we play late into the night,
At times it's right after school.

This part of our lives is dedicated,
To following after kids.
The tricky part is maintaining contact,
So relationships don't hit the skids.

As long as we both understand,
There is life after this.
These years will fly by like a flash,
And it's back to wedded bliss.

Sports Rage

This person comes to the game upset,
Everything makes him mad.
He yells negative things at the team,
His response to officials is really bad.

I'm waiting for this guy to explode,
Maybe have a heart attack or stroke.
His face turns red, he spits and sputters,
He's at risk and that's no joke.

I wish he could see what that does to the kid,
When he just won't settle down.
The pressure he exhibits is contagious,
You can watch it spread around.

I know he cares about his child,
He cares about the sport.
By yelling less and cheering more,
He could really display support.

What role do we play while in the stands,
As fans we should evaluate.
Is winning more important than everything,
Or is it the support and sportsmanship we create?

54
RAH

Cheers

Something one learns early on,
Is to never yell "sweetie" or "honey".
Your poor child will never forgive you,
On that you can bet money.

In trying to keep the spirits up,
Some times a Mom gets excited.
She may speak up if her child gets hurt,
Or even louder if she's delighted.

Out slip those little endearments,
That should be only used in private.
Regardless of our child's shape or size,
They are still our baby—you bet.

Just add a hug to go with the term,
And you are really guaranteed to please.
A big smooch on the cheek,
And you can bring them to their knees.

Kids don't really mind it,
Though they will quickly pass the blame.
Kissing them in front of friends,
Is really, really lame!

BLEACHER
BUDDIES

T-shirts

Kids are coming to the bleachers,
With their hands out for some cash.
They want to buy a T-shirt,
To add to their stash.

At every invitational,
And tournament home and away,
There is a special T-shirt,
To commemorate the day.

Some have logos using humor,
Some celebrate the sport.
You get a free one for attending camp,
Colors and styles of every sort.

T-shirts are a history,
Of fun had at an event.
They provide a stimulus for memories,
Long after we've forgotten money spent.

The bleacher buddies do agree,
As the piles grow on the shelf.
"If your name is on the T-shirt,
Please behave yourself!"

28
Pep Rally
8:00pm
29
Final
Game
7:30 pm
30

Season Ending

As the season comes to an end,
There is a huge sense of relief.
Also I'm feeling something else,
Could this feeling be grief?

How could feelings be so mixed?
I really should be glad.
No more running, or full weekends,
Why do I feel so sad?

I'll miss the kids and action,
I'll miss my bleacher buddies, too.
I'll miss the calendar full to the brim,
But I have lots of things to do.

Maybe I'll get that closet cleaned,
Or make a family meal.
Maybe I'll finish that project:
How would a nice long bath really feel?

This has become our way of life,
Running from sport to sport.
At one time the season seemed so long,
And now it seems so short.

BLEACHER BUDDIES

Making Memories

How can I tell my buddies goodbye,
Whether until next year or forever.
I want them to know how much I care,
And that I'll forget them never.

Maybe a little book would help,
To tell them how I feel.
I could get my buddies to sign it,
That should be no big deal.

As we sit there during final play,
Or wave and meet and greet.
We could talk and laugh about the poems,
That would be really neat!

This book could be the perfect thing,
To keep the memories alive.
Of many hours of watching sports,
We thought we'd never survive.

Whether just starting out as buddies,
Or bleacher mates for many years.
It's a special group of people,
Sharing laughter, fun and tears.